Rocks and Minerals

THIS EDITION
Editorial Management by Oriel Square
Produced for DK by WonderLab Group LLC
Jennifer Emmett, Erica Green, Kate Hale, *Founders*

Editors Grace Hill Smith, Libby Romero, Maya Myers, Michaela Weglinski;
Photography Editors Kelley Miller, Annette Kiesow, Nicole DiMella; **Managing Editor** Rachel Houghton;
Designers Project Design Company; **Researcher** Michelle Harris; **Copy Editor** Lori Merritt;
Indexer Connie Binder; **Proofreader** Larry Shea; **Reading Specialist** Dr. Jennifer Albro;
Curriculum Specialist Elaine Larson

Published in the United States by DK Publishing
1745 Broadway, 20th Floor, New York, NY 10019
Copyright © 2023 Dorling Kindersley Limited
DK, a Division of Penguin Random House LLC
23 24 25 26 10 9 8 7 6 5 4 3 2 1
001-333863-Oct/2023

A catalog record for this book
is available from the Library of Congress.
HC ISBN: 978-0-7440-7116-0
PB ISBN: 978-0-7440-7130-6

DK books are available at special discounts when purchased in bulk for sales promotions, premiums,
fundraising, or educational use. For details, contact: DK Publishing Special Markets,
1745 Broadway, 20th Floor, New York, NY 10019
SpecialSales@dk.com

Printed and bound in China

The publisher would like to thank the following for their kind permission to reproduce their images:
a=above; c=center; b=below; l=left; r=right; t=top; b/g=background

123RF.com: Amy Harris 19tr, www.amphoto.lt / Audrius Merfeldas 44cl; **Alamy Stock Photo:** David Fleetham 16tl,
Fabiano Caddeo Goreme 38br, PS-I 41bl, SBS Eclectic Images 42br, Science History Images 34tl, The Natural History Museum 43cl,
Matthijs Wetterauw 4-5, Ajith Perera / Xinhua 42tl; **Dorling Kindersley:** Richard Leeney / Holts Gems, Hatton Garden 33crb,
42clb (blue gem), Ruth Jenkinson / Holts Gems 39cr, 40clb, Harry Taylor / Natural History Museum, London 18tl, Tim Parmenter /
Natural History Museum, London 42clb (red gem); **Dreamstime.com:** Alexkar08 26tl, Allison14 10cla, Kostyantyn Babenko 6-7t,
Jeffrey Banke 36cla, 37tr, Bartkowski 21tr, Thanasak Boonchoong 28br, Carlosphotos 45br, Chernetskaya 16clb, Dary423 36tl,
εμ ® 32clb, Demerzel21 21bl, Lynda Dobbin Turner 38cl, Catherine Downie 26br, Fosna13 30t, Gardendreamer 8clb, Glebtarro 24b,
Tomas Griger 23bl, Andrey Gudkov 11tr, Happystock 31c, David Hayes 37crb, 37bl, Irishgold 18cla, Jckca 44bl, Roberto Junior 29cr, Lars
Kastilan 18bl, Kelpfish 23cra, Vichaya Kiatyingangsule 3b, Oleksandr Kostiuchenko 39bc, Luis Louro 41cra, Luckyphotographer 24tl,
Maxironwas 25cl, Olga Mendenhall 20tl, Montree Nanta 33tr, Noiral 43tr, James Phelps 14-15, Photogolfer 20cla, Daniel Prudek 22tl,
Pytyczech 7br, Salajean 30-31, Martin Schneiter 22br, Yury Shirokov / Yuris 44tl, Smartyunknown 28tl, Stephen Tapply 19bl, Romolo
Tavani 8tl, Nikhil Gangavane / Thefinalmiracle 39tr, Jiri Vaclavek 1b, Vvoevale 12cl, Kevin Walker 9, Wavebreakmedia Ltd 44-45t, Bjrn
Wylezich 33cra (br), 35tr, Xenomanes 27tr, Xtremepixel 6tl, Bing Bing Zhu 39cl; **Getty Images:** 500Px Plus / Sharif Uddin 17br, Digital
Vision / Thomas Northcut 38tl, Moment Open / Simon Emmett Photography 29tl, Ratnakorn Piyasirisorost 31tr, Alex Wong / Staff
42cb; **Getty Images / iStock:** badboydt7 10tl, E+ / kickstand 45tr, Flory 19cr, mtcurado 11l, RuslanDashinsky 41crb, Sjo 18br,
SusanWoodImages 30bl, VvoeVale 32tl; **Science Photo Library:** Dr Juerg Alean 27bl, Andrew Lambert Photography 35tl, Ted
Kinsman 34cr, 34br, Prof. Stewart Lowther 16br, Javier Trueba / MSF 40tl, Science Stock Photography 27br, Michael Szoenyi 17bl,
Dirk Wiersma 13l, 36br; **Shutterstock.com:** Christopher Meder 13tr, NNNMMM 17tr, thanmano 35cr

Cover images: *Front:* **Dorling Kindersley:** Ruth Jenkinson / Holts Gems bl, Gary Ombler,
Oxford University Museum of Natural History

All other images © Dorling Kindersley
For more information see: www.dkimages.com

For the curious
www.dk.com

Rocks and Minerals

Brenna Maloney

CONTENTS

Geologist
A scientist who studies and identifies rocks is called a geologist.

"Living" Rocks
Some kinds of rock are not made of minerals. They are formed from living things. Coal is a rock that's made from plant material. Amber is made from ancient tree resin. Jet is a rock made from dead wood that has hardened.

WHAT ARE ROCKS AND MINERALS?

Rocks have incredible stories to share. They help tell the story of our planet. Over millions of years, rocks go on a journey from deep inside Earth to the surface and back inside Earth again. We can learn a lot about our planet just by studying them. But we have to know what to look for. Let's start by understanding what rocks are.

Rocks are the pebbles that you pick up from a stream or a mountain that you climb. Rocks are everywhere! They can be smooth or rough, light or heavy, gray or colorful.

Almost all rocks are made of minerals. Minerals are solid materials found in nature that are not made by plants, animals, or other living things. You might sprinkle one mineral on your food: halite, or salt, is a mineral!

THREE TYPES OF ROCKS

Geologists classify rocks according to how they form. There are three types of rocks: igneous, sedimentary, and metamorphic.

Igneous Rock

Deep within Earth, temperatures are hot enough to melt rock. This molten rock is called magma. Magma either pools in underground chambers or it rises to the surface and erupts. When magma breaks through the surface, it's called lava. When lava cools, it hardens into igneous rock.

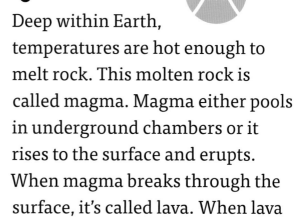

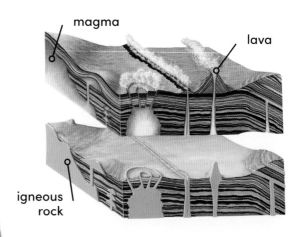

magma

lava

igneous rock

Igneous

There are more than 700 types of igneous rocks, and they are generally the hardest and heaviest of all rocks.

Devils Tower in Wyoming, USA, is made of igneous rock.

Sandstone
The Rainbow Mountains in Gansu, China, are formed from sandstone, a sedimentary rock.

Drawings
Infrared photography revealed more information about prehistoric drawings on the sandstone in Arches National Park in Utah, USA.

Sediment
The word "sediment" comes from the Latin words *sedimentum*, meaning "settling," and *sedēre*, "to sink down."

Sedimentary Rock

Sedimentary rocks are formed from pieces of existing rock. How? Rocks weather, or break down, into smaller pieces. Then, the pieces of rock, called sediment, are carried away by rain and wind. The sediment is washed or blown into oceans, valleys, and riverbeds. It collects, building up in layers. Over time, these layers become so tightly compacted that they form solid rock.

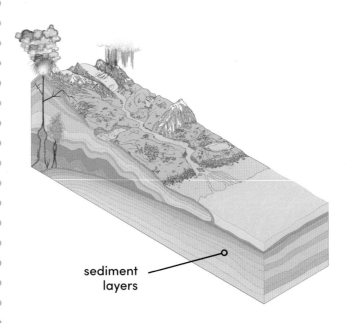

sediment layers

Tsingy de Bemaraha

The razor-sharp, limestone spires in Tsingy de Bemaraha Strict Nature Reserve are difficult for people to navigate, but sifakas, a type of lemur, easily leap across them.

The grand karst limestone formation in Tsingy de Bemaraha Strict Nature Reserve near the western coast of Madagascar is made of sedimentary rock.

Metamorphic

Metamorphic rocks get their name from the words *meta*, meaning "change," and *morphē*, meaning "form."

Protolith

A protolith is the original rock from which a metamorphic rock is formed.

Eclogites

Eclogites are red and green metamorphic or igneous rocks. The color of these rare rocks comes from the presence of two minerals, red garnet and green pyroxene. Eclogite is sometimes called the "Christmas rock" because of its colors.

Metamorphic Rocks

Earth's crust, or surface, is made up of huge pieces of rock that fit together like a giant jigsaw puzzle. When these plates move, they transform existing rocks into new rocks. These new rocks are called metamorphic rocks. Most metamorphic rocks form deep inside Earth. Over time, they are pushed up to the surface.

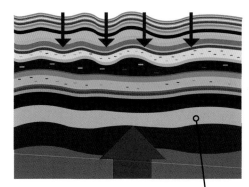

heat and pressure

metamorphic rocks

Jasper, a variety of chalcedony, is metamorphic rock. This rock formation is in the middle of the West Australian desert.

Soapstone
Because soapstone is soft and easy to carve, this metamorphic rock has been used to make bowls and art for thousands of years.

Hornfels
When a pool of magma heats the surrounding rocks, these rocks undergo a process called contact metamorphism. They are transformed into hornfels, a type of metamorphic rock. Hornfels are dense and hard to break.

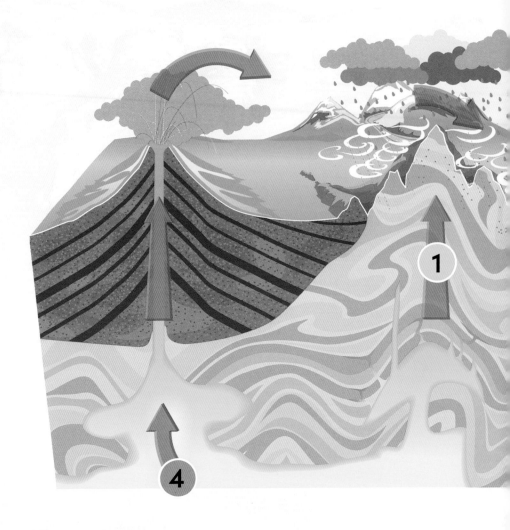

THE ROCK CYCLE

Rocks on Earth are recycled. That means that rocks don't stay the same. Over thousands of years, they change. This process, when one type of rock is transformed into another, is called the rock cycle.

Turn the page to take a look at different types of igneous, sedimentary, and metamorphic rocks.

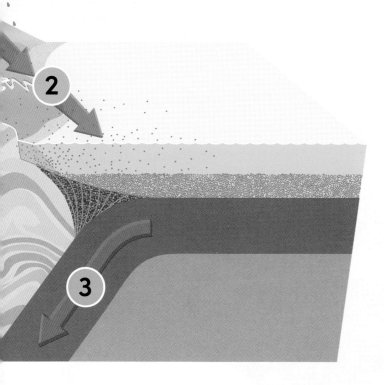

1 Molten rock deep inside Earth can cool, hardening into igneous rock. Molten rock inside Earth can also erupt, hardening into igneous rock on Earth's surface.

2 Rain and wind slowly break down these rocks into pieces, or sediment. Erosion carries the sediment away and deposits it, often into water, where it is compressed into sedimentary rock.

3 Over time, sedimentary rocks can be driven back below Earth's surface. Sedimentary rocks are heated and squeezed, eventually becoming metamorphic rocks.

4 Then, these metamorphic rocks melt to form magma, which eventually can become igneous rocks. The rock cycle begins all over again.

Pumice Raft
Eruptions of underwater volcanoes can create a floating patch, or raft, of pumice. An example of this can be seen around the Tonga islands in the Pacific Ocean.

Skin Care
Some people use pumice for skin care. The rough texture of a pumice stone can be used to remove dead skin.

PUMICE

Pumice can float on water! It forms when superheated, pressurized molten rock bursts from a volcano as lava. Gases in the melted rock form bubbles when the pressure suddenly decreases—similar to how bubbles spurt out when you shake and then open a carbonated drink. The lava quickly cools, producing a rock filled with air pockets.

Pumice is considered a volcanic glass because the lava that forms it cools so quickly that crystals—the repeating shapes that make up most minerals—can't form.

When Mount St. Helens in Washington State, USA, erupted in 1980, lava cooled into pumice, covering the ground.

PELE'S HAIR

Don't be fooled by the look of these soft, wispy fibers. They aren't hair! These long, fragile strands are made of volcanic glass. Pele's hair is created when lava cools rapidly in midair. Strands may be up to a couple feet long, but each one is extremely thin. Because they are so light, they are carried by the wind. They can collect on the ground and form thick mats. These glass fibers are brittle and sharp.

Goddess Pele
Pele's hair was named after the Hawaiian goddess of fire. According to legend, she lived in the Kilauea volcano. When her bad temper became explosive, Kilauea erupted.

Birds' Nests
Some birds make their nests with Pele's hair.

Mount Hekla
Obsidian can be found near Mount Hekla in Iceland and on the Aeolian Islands in Italy.

Obsidian Cliff
Most obsidian is found as small rocks, but Obsidian Cliff in Yellowstone National Park, USA, is a tall formation.

Ancient Mirrors
The Aztec civilization used obsidian for mirrors.

OBSIDIAN

Like pumice, obsidian is a volcanic glass that forms when lava cools rapidly. It is commonly found near volcanoes, at the edges of lava flows, and in places where lava entered a lake or sea.

When obsidian is broken, its pieces can have sharp edges. Because of this, obsidian was once used to make weapons and tools. It is used today in heart surgery. Obsidian blades have a cutting edge many times sharper than steel surgical scalpels.

Mount Hekla, Iceland

TUFF

Tuff forms during an explosive volcanic eruption. Ash, pieces of rock, and lava are ejected into the air. As they fall to the ground, they mix and stick together, hardening into rock. Tuff is relatively soft and porous. It has been used as a building material since ancient times because it is easy to work with.

These enormous statues on Easter Island are made out of tuff.

Mystery
No one knows who made the statues on Easter Island or why, but scientists do know that they were carved between A.D. 1200 and 1500.

Pompeii
When Mount Vesuvius erupted in 79 CE, destroying the city of Pompeii, Italy, tuff formed. It created a shell around the people and objects trapped under the ash, preserving a moment in time.

Mount Rushmore
The granite that forms Mount Rushmore in South Dakota is among the oldest in the western United States.

El Capitan
El Capitan, a granite rock formation in Yosemite National Park, USA, formed underground. Millions of years ago, the movement of tectonic plates forced the rocks upward. El Capitan is about 3,000 feet (914 m) from base to summit along its tallest face.

GRANITE

Granite can be found on every continent on Earth. Granite forms when magma cools slowly underground. Over millions of years, rain and wind wear away the rocks and soil on Earth's surface, exposing the granite.

Granite often has a coarse texture because of the slow cooling process, which allows the rock's minerals to form larger crystals. You might recognize this rock because it's used to make many objects found in our daily lives, such as countertops, floor tiles, and paving stones.

BASALT

Basalt is a hard, black rock. It forms from lava that cools rapidly at Earth's surface. When lava cools underwater, it creates pillow-shaped bodies of rock.

Basalt is the primary rock in Earth's oceanic crust. Basalt is also an abundant rock on the Moon. It is a common rock on the planets Venus and Mars, too.

Giant's Causeway Thousands of basalt columns make up Giant's Causeway in Northern Ireland.

Ripple Effect Basalt lava can also form in ripples. It's called pahoehoe (puh-ho-ee-ho-ee) basalt.

Basalt rock formation in south Iceland

LIMESTONE

There are many different kinds of limestone, but they all form in water.

One type of limestone forms in warm, shallow waters. Shells from animals like oysters and clams break down into tiny pieces. Layers of these pieces, called lime, build up and eventually form limestone.

Another type of limestone forms in caves. Stalactites are icicle-like mineral deposits on a cave's ceiling, left behind when water drips down. Stalagmites are pillar-like mineral deposits on a cave's floor, formed when water drips down and the minerals pile up.

Stalactites and stalagmites in Carlsbad Caverns, New Mexico, USA

CHALK

This white or light gray rock is a form of limestone. It forms from a fine-grained marine sediment known as ooze. When marine algae or other organisms die, their remains sink to the bottom of the seafloor and accumulate. Over time, layers of ooze compress and form rock. Chalk is often powdery and brittle.

The White Cliffs of Dover, England, are made of chalk.

School Chalk
Chalk was once used in classrooms to write on blackboards. Sidewalk chalk that is used today is made from a different material.

Playing Field
Chalk has been used to mark playing fields for sports such as soccer and baseball.

SANDSTONE

Sandstone is made up of sand-size grains of minerals and other rocks. Wind, water, or ice carry the grains to depressions, or low-lying areas, in Earth's crust. Over time, the pieces are compacted and cemented into rock. Sandstone is one of the most common types of sedimentary rock.

Ripples
Ripples in sandstone can indicate the direction of local water currents or wind.

Vermilion Cliffs National Monument, Arizona, USA

COAL

Coal is another kind of sedimentary rock. It forms when dead plants build up on the bottom of swamps. Layers of sediment and dirt cover the plants. Over millions of years, the resulting pressure and heat turn the plants into rock. Coal can burn. It can be used to create heat and electricity.

Energy Source
Coal is called a fossil fuel because it is made from the fossils of plants.

Most coal is found underground.

Lignite
Lignite is a type of coal. Unlike coal, plant materials can still be seen in this soft rock. Also unlike coal, lignite is found near Earth's surface.

Thick Rocks
Masses of marble can be several hundred feet thick.

MARBLE

Over time, high heat and intense pressure underground change limestone, a sedimentary rock, into marble, a metamorphic rock. Calcite, a mineral that helped form the original limestone, recrystallizes to form a denser rock.

In its purest form, marble is sparkling white. But, sometimes, different types of minerals can give marble a pink, brown, gray, or green color. Marble has long been used for sculptures and as a building material.

Veins
The lines that sometimes run through marble are called veins.

Taj Mahal, India

GNEISS

Gneiss can form from granite, an igneous rock. Gneiss is typically found buried deep in many mountain ranges. Here, rock such as granite is subjected to great pressures and temperatures. Over time, these forces alter the chemical composition of the rock.

Gneiss is abundant on the lower level of Earth's crust.

Say My Name
Gneiss is pronounced "nice."

Old Rock
One of the oldest rocks on Earth is a piece of gneiss that was found in an isolated region of Canada's Northwest Territories. It is believed to be more than four billion years old.

Crystals
The eye-shaped spots on augen gneiss are large mineral crystals in the rock.

Petrified
Petrification is the most common method of fossilization. Minerals replace the organic material, and the remains are turned into stone or "petrified."

Compressed
A compression fossil forms when plant or animal remains are compressed under the weight of sediment and water.

FOSSILS

Fossils are the remains of living things that have been preserved in rocks. Sedimentary rocks like sandstone, shale, and limestone make good homes for fossils. Fossils give scientists helpful clues about the history of life on Earth. They can tell us how our planet has changed over millions of years.

Scientists use a brush to help expose a fossil covered by sand.

©Esperanza Photography

Mold
When a shell or bone has dissolved, it may leave behind a shape of the animal. This shape is called a mold.

Remains like shells, bones, and teeth are buried under sediment. Mineral-rich water filters through the sediment. As more and more sediment builds up, it creates pressure that starts to turn the layers into rock. The bones or other remains harden in the sediment, creating a fossil.

Preserved
The rarest form of fossilization is preserved remains. The original skeletons and soft body parts of a living thing are intact.

Over time, Earth's tectonic plates shift, lifting fossils up to the surface. Fossils are almost always found in sedimentary rocks. The heat and pressure that create metamorphic or igneous rocks usually destroy any fossils.

REMARKABLE ROCKS

Earth is a dynamic place, and evidence of how rocks transform its landscape can be seen all around us.

Uluru

One of Australia's most celebrated natural landmarks is the world's largest sandstone monolith, a massive formation composed of a single rock or stone. Uluru rises 1,142 feet (348 m) above the otherwise flat landscape of the Australian Outback. This rock is called an inselberg, or isolated mountain. Inselbergs are the remnants left behind after the erosion of a mountain range.

Moeraki Boulders

More than 50 spherical stones are scattered across a stretch of Koekohe Beach in New Zealand. Each boulder weighs several tons and is up to 6.5 feet (2 m) high. These rocks started forming in seafloor sediment about 65 million years ago and became exposed through shoreline erosion.

Danxia

China's Danxia landform looks as if it has been painted with a brush. Layers of spectacularly colored sandstone and minerals were pressed together more than 24 million years ago. Tectonic plate activity buckled these layers, which were further shaped by wind and rain. Over time, erosion exposed natural pillars, towers, ravines, and valleys.

Shilin

Some 270 million years ago, this stone forest in China was covered by an ancient sea. Layer upon layer of shells and calcified marine life slowly transformed into limestone and dolomite. Wind, rain, and time then sculpted extraordinary shapes with varying colors, patterns, and sizes to create today's stone labyrinth.

MORE ON MINERALS

Most rocks are made up of one or more minerals. Minerals are inorganic substances. That means they are made of nonliving things.

Most minerals are made up of repeating shapes called crystals. Each mineral has its own shape. The flat faces of crystals can be squares, rectangles, triangles, diamonds, or hexagons. Pyrite, for example, has a cubic crystal shape. Quartz can have a hexagonal crystal shape.

Minerals have physical properties. These include crystal shape, color, luster, cleavage, streak, and hardness. These are characteristics that we can see and test using simple methods.

Sulfur is yellow. Graphite is black. But some minerals can be more than one color. Quartz, for example, can be white, yellow, purple, and pink.

Types of Minerals
There are more than 5,000 types of minerals on Earth.

Mineralogy
The study of minerals is called mineralogy.

Luster refers to how shiny a mineral is. Some minerals, like copper and zinc, have a metallic luster. Talc is described as "pearly." Other words to describe luster are "glassy" or "dull."

Cleavage describes the way a mineral splits when it is struck. This natural splitting usually follows the pattern of the mineral's crystal shape.

When a mineral is rubbed across a piece of unglazed porcelain, it leaves a colored powder. This is known as the mineral's streak. The streak is not always the same color as the mineral.

A mineral's hardness refers to how well it resists scratching. It is measured using a chart called the Mohs Hardness Scale. The scale ranges from 1 to 10, with 1 being the softest and 10 being the hardest. Talc is the softest mineral, and lonsdaleite is the hardest.

Psilomelane (dull)

Limonite
(earthy)

Asbestos (silky)

Tourmaline
(glassy)

Galena (metallic)

Magnetic Minerals

Some minerals are attracted to magnetic fields, but there is only one mineral that acts like a magnet: lodestone. Pieces of lodestone served as the first magnetic compasses and were used in China as early as 300 BCE.

OTHER PROPERTIES OF MINERALS

Some minerals have additional properties that help mineralogists identify them.

Some minerals absorb ultraviolet light. This is a type of light that our eyes cannot detect. These minerals fluoresce, or glow in the dark when exposed to ultraviolet light. Calcite can fluoresce in several colors.

Diopside under regular light

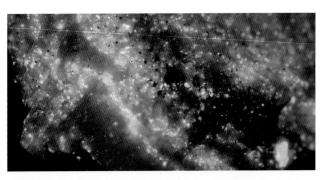

Diopside under ultraviolet light flouresces

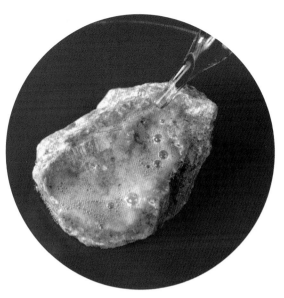

Limestone fizzes with hydrochloric acid.

Some minerals release radioactive energy. This energy cannot be seen, heard, or felt, but it can be recorded with a Geiger counter. Uranium and thorium are both radioactive minerals.

Some minerals can be identified based on their reaction to acid. The calcite in limestone, for example, fizzes when an acid is applied to the rock.

Some minerals emit odors. Sulfur gives off an odor that resembles a lighted match. If heated, sulfur smells of rotten eggs.

Sulfur
Sulfur is often found near volcanoes. In its pure form, sulfur has bright yellow crystals.

Colorful Eruption
When sulfur gases erupt from the Kawah Ijen volcano in Indonesia, they combine with the air and explode into blue flames.

All the Gold
Worldwide, it's estimated that the total amount of gold ever mined is enough to fill 60 tractor trailers.

Gold Rush
Gold is one of the heaviest minerals. It sinks and collects at the bottom of streams. People hurried to California, USA, in 1848 to pan for gold.

In Our Veins
Gold makes up about 0.02 percent of our blood.

GOLD

Few minerals have the importance of gold. Like most metals, gold can conduct heat and electricity. But it's also so pliable that it can be made into sewing thread. Gold is a nonreactive metal and does not rust. It was one of the first forms of money and has been valued since ancient times for its beauty. Gold can appear as shiny stripes or large nuggets inside of rocks.

Gold on quartzite

PYRITE

Pyrite is so often mistaken for gold that it has earned the nickname "Fool's Gold." This mineral's color and metallic luster are deceptively gold-like. But, to the trained eye, these minerals are very different. Gold is soft; pyrite is hard. That means that gold can be molded or bent, while thin pieces of pyrite will break. When gold is scraped against a surface, it leaves a yellow streak, but pyrite leaves a greenish black streak.

Firestarter
Pyrite is named after the Greek word *pyr* meaning "fire." Pyrite can be used to create the sparks needed for starting a fire if it is struck against metal or another hard material.

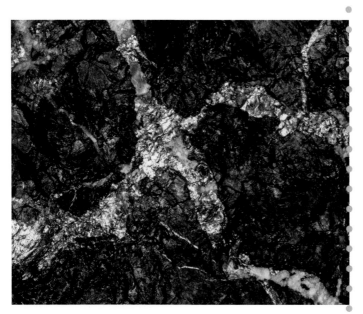

Pyrite in a bed of black lead ore

Stinky Smell
Gold has no odor, but pyrite gives off a sulfurous smell (like rotten eggs)!

It's Electric!
Quartz has a unique electrical property. It is widely used in electronics. Radios, microphones, robotics, clocks, watches, and many more electronic devices use quartz crystals.

Fulgurites
When lightning strikes sand, its intense heat can form fulgurites, or hollow glass tubes. Their shape mimics the path of the lightning bolt as it scatters into the ground.

QUARTZ

Quartz is the most abundant mineral in Earth's crust. It can be found in many types of igneous, sedimentary, and metamorphic rocks. You might find it right under your toes at the beach, as quartz crystals are often found in sand. When sand that contains a lot of quartz is melted, it can be molded into glass!

The unique properties of quartz make it one of the most useful natural substances. Quartz is commonly used in glassmaking, in the petroleum industry, as an abrasive, as a building material, and even as a gemstone.

MALACHITE

Malachite is a mineral that can form in caves near another mineral, copper. Water and copper combine to form malachite. It is distinctive for its deep green color. Throughout history, malachite has been used to make jewelry and sculptures. It can also be ground into a powder to make green paint.

Evil Spirits
In ancient Greece and Rome, malachite was worn as jewelry to ward off evil spirits.

Bubbly
Unlike many minerals, malachite rarely forms crystals. It can have a bubbly surface.

Giant Gypsum
One type of gypsum, called selenite gypsum, is found in the Cave of the Crystals near Naica, Chihuahua, Mexico. Huge crystals form icicle-like shapes.

Pretty "Petals"
Another type of gypsum, desert rose gypsum, forms in a flower-like shape.

GYPSUM

Gypsum is a common mineral that has been used as a building material since ancient times. Today, it is used in construction as drywall, wallboard, sheetrock, or plasterboard. It can also be used as a fertilizer. This versatile mineral is used in foot creams, shampoos, and other hair products, too.

Gypsum forms when ocean or salty lake water dries up. The water leaves deposits behind that can form into gypsum crystals.

HALITE

Halite is the only mineral that people eat. Most of us know it by another name: salt. Salt comes from the sea and from solid layers underground. Halite crystals form when salty water evaporates. People also use salt to de-ice roads and highways in the winter. They use salt as a water softener or as a food preserver. Salt is also used in the paper industry to process wood fibers.

Pass the Salt
Salt is one of the oldest and most common food seasonings.

Money Mineral
Roman soldiers were paid with salt as well as gold.

Crystallized salt formations along the shores of the Dead Sea, Israel

Dead Sea
The high concentration of salt in the Dead Sea makes the water so dense that you can't swim. You can only float!

Large Crystal
The largest single corundum crystal ever recorded weighed around 335 pounds (152 kg).

CORUNDUM

Corundum is a very hard mineral—a nine on the Mohs scale! Corundum in its pure state is colorless. But, in the presence of small amounts of impurities, its color can change. For example, when corundum mixes with chromium, its color changes to red—becoming a ruby. When it mixes with iron and titanium, it turns blue—becoming a sapphire.

Rare Gems
Corundum is not difficult to find, but rubies and sapphires are rare. They are often polished and cut to make jewelry.

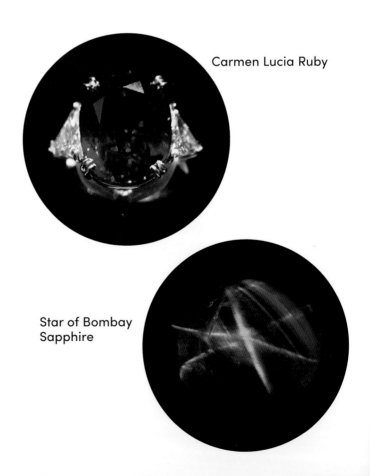

Carmen Lucia Ruby

Star of Bombay Sapphire

DIAMOND

Diamond, the second hardest mineral on Earth, is made of pure carbon. Diamonds form under high pressure and high temperature, and they take millions of years to form. Volcanic eruptions bring diamonds to Earth's surface in igneous rocks known as kimberlites.

Indestructible
The word "diamond" comes from the Greek word *adamas.* It means "invincible" or "indestructible."

Hard Minerals
Lonsdaleite is the only mineral that is harder than diamond. Both minerals are made of carbon.

Uncut and cut diamond

Scratch Test
The only substance that can scratch a diamond is another diamond.

All Around Us
We use rocks
and minerals
in our lives
every day.

Batteries:
lead, lithium

Computer chips:
silicon

Jeans: pumice
(to distress
the denim)

PROTECTING OUR RESOURCES

We can't live without rocks and
minerals! Through them, we learn
about our planet. We use these
vital resources in our everyday
lives. They also help us develop
new technologies.

Toothpaste: fluoride, pumice, titanium dioxide

Mirrors: silver

Plant pots: clay, mudstone

Because rocks and minerals are nonrenewable resources—they take millions of years to form and can't be replaced during a person's lifetime—we need to use them responsibly. We want to take care of our planet so that all living things can benefit from rocks and minerals now and in the future.

Fireworks: sulfur

GLOSSARY

Crystal
The special shape that a mineral takes

Erosion
The movement of weathered rock and sediment by wind, water, or ice (glaciers)

Evaporate
To change a liquid into a vapor or gas

Fluoresce
To glow under ultraviolet light

Fossil
The preserved remains or traces of a living organism

Geologist
A scientist who studies Earth's structure and its history through rocks and minerals

Igneous rock
A rock formed though the cooling of magma or lava

Inorganic
Not consisting of, or deriving from, living matter

Lava
Molten rock that is expelled to Earth's surface by a volcano

Magma
Molten rock that is under Earth's surface

Metamorphic rock
A rock that is changed by intense heat and/or pressure into another type of rock

Mineralogy
The scientific study of minerals

Monolith
A large, single upright block of stone

Organic
Made up of materials that were once living

Radioactive
Emitting or relating to the emission of ionizing radiation or particles

Rock cycle
The continual process where "new" rocks are made from rocks that already existed

Sediment
Any material that results from weathering or decomposition and is carried by erosion to bodies of water where it settles on the bottom

Sedimentary rock
Rocks formed when layers of sediment are pressed and cemented together

Tectonic plate
A large section of Earth's crust that moves

Volcano
An opening in the crust through which molten rock (magma) erupts to the surface as lava

INDEX

QUIZ

Answer the questions to see what you have learned. Check your answers in the key below.

1. What type of rock forms when pieces of rock are compressed into layers?

2. What is the name for scientists who study rocks?

3. How do igneous rocks form?

4. Which rock can float on water?

5. What type of rock is coal?

6. What type of rock lands on Earth from space?

7. What is Earth's most common mineral?

8. What type of rock forms when existing rock is changed by extreme heat or pressure?

1. Sedimentary 2. Geologist 3. By molten rock cooling 4. Pumice
5. Sedimentary 6. Meteorite 7. Quartz 8. Metamorphic